One Week at a Time

Grounded and Growing
Through His Word

DALE HANSEN

WESTBOW
PRESS®
A DIVISION OF THOMAS NELSON
& ZONDERVAN

WestBow Press books may be ordered through booksellers or by contacting:

WestBow Press
A Division of Thomas Nelson & Zondervan
1663 Liberty Drive
Bloomington, IN 47403
www.westbowpress.com
1 (866) 928-1240

ISBN: 978-1-5127-9768-8 (sc)
ISBN: 978-1-5127-9769-5 (e)

Library of Congress Control Number: 2017911921

Print information available on the last page.

WestBow Press rev. date: 7/31/2017

To my friends who have impacted my life for Christ:

Patti, my wife of more than forty years and
my encourager and supporter.
Mike, who challenged and developed me as a leader and a teacher.
Denis, who strengthened my Biblical foundations as a young believer.
Arnold, who encouraged me with many one-on-one times.
Wayne, who helped me grow spiritually as my pastor and friend.
Dennis, who encourages life change as my current pastor and friend.

Introduction

One Week at a Time came together as I thought of working on one devotion or one study at a time. Spending a week in the same verses, instructions, and application, could help you make fifty-two changes in your life. Realistically, this could help make many changes over a period of time. Reading His Word is important, but we can get caught up in how many verses we read each day.

As we read and study His Word, our goal will be to know Him more. Jeremiah tells us God wants us to only boast in understanding and knowing Him (Jeremiah 9:23–24). Our relationship with Him must be our top priority.

This book will allow you to work on one reading and one application per week. Each week includes an "Overview," a "Focus" and a "How to Apply" section. Over the course of fifty-two weeks, the key applications will include the following challenges:

- reading His Word daily
- keeping a prayer list to track requests
- listing verses to use in prayer
- evaluating changes in areas of your life
- knowing God better and obeying Him
- controlling your thoughts, words, and actions
- intentionally taking charge of your walk with God

I have heard the challenge to move forward in your walk with God and to be a doer and not just a hearer (James 1:22). This is like driving a car. If your life is parked on the side of the road, you will go nowhere. If you are driving out on the road, you will make progress. You may not always be in the correct lane, but God can guide and steer a moving car. He will never be able to move or steer a parked car. Remember that He is in the driver's seat.

I hope this book challenges you like it challenged me as I wrote the lessons. Work on these by yourself, with a partner, or in a group. Many of these applications have helped my family work through opportunities, including parenthood, cancer, infertility, job changes, relocations, kidney stones, and Parkinson's.

Wishing for all the growth with you!

WEEK 1

2 Timothy 1:1–18
Focus: 1:7

Overview: Paul was thankful for Timothy's sincere faith. We are saved through Christ's grace, through His death, and for His purpose. We should not be ashamed of Christ and His gospel. He challenges Timothy to continue with sound teaching and in tune with the Holy Spirit who is in us.

Focus: In verse 7, Timothy was young and may have lacked confidence to step forward into action. Discipline is action—doing and allowing God to work in and through us. He does not want us to be timid; instead, God wants us to be bold through power, love, and self-discipline.

How to Apply: Our actions to move forward can include the following:

- making a big decision
- deciding between good and best
- deciding to do what is right
- taking your spouse on a date
- reaching out to a friend via phone call, note, or text
- removing or reducing a distraction (TV, hobbies, etc.)
- committing to praying five minutes a day to start
- picking at least one of the above to work on this week

WEEK 2

Ephesians 3:1–21
Focus: 3:20

Overview: Paul prays for the Ephesians to be rooted, grounded, and anchored in God's love and power. We need to work on knowing that His love for us surpasses what we believe love is. Paul mentions how God's grace is in Him, and Paul is able to share the gospel to all people. All the glory is to God the Father with His eternal purpose accomplished through Jesus Christ, the Son.

Focus: In verse 20, we can do more than we could dream, desire, imagine, or ask for. We can do all this through His power working in us. We must ask God to work in His way and not through our plans. Every day, we can see Him working and answering our prayers in a powerful way.

How to Apply: See how God can use you this week in one of the examples below:

- asking for His help in making a decision
- asking Him for us not to limit His work through us
- reaching out to a friend who we believe is unreachable
- asking Him for help with something you do not have enough confidence to do yourself
- memorize Ephesians 3:20

WEEK 3

Jeremiah 29:1–23
Focus: 29:11

Overview: The people of Israel are in exile in Babylon, and God promises to free them. If they seek and find Him, He has plans for them to prosper. He will restore them to their land physically and restore them to Him spiritually.

Focus: In verse 11, Israel has a hope and future in Him. Like Israel in captivity, our current circumstances may cause us to doubt that He is with us. Yet after the people of Israel spent some time in exile, God brought them back to the promised land. It is the same with us. At times, we feel like we are alone, yet we will return to Him and be aware of His presence again, despite our circumstances.

How to Apply: Our challenge is to ensure that we are seeking His plans for our lives and obeying Him. Our hope and future are in Him as we call upon Him. Decide to pray through your current circumstances and look beyond to your future plans. Pray each day this week for His plan and His perspective. Put a prayer list together with current issues and potential future plans.

WEEK 4

Galatians 6:1–18
Focus: 6:9

Overview: Paul cautions the Galatians to be aware of their own actions and to stop trying to compare themselves to others. Paul tells them that their actions should be in obedience to Him and not be influenced by their sinful nature. Their influence should be through His Spirit. The same is for us today. In pleasing our sinful nature, the result will be to reap destruction. When we seek to please God's Spirit, the result is eternal life.

Focus: In verse 9, Paul challenges us not to give up in doing good and to look forward to the harvest we will reap someday. Be intentional to seek God's Spirit. Let us not give up on:

- a struggling relationship
- a current job situation
- raising our children
- home life
- finances
- church

How to Apply: At times, we will need to seek His perspective and decide to intentionally follow Him. Throughout this week, pray with the prayer list from last week. Include any opportunities where God directs you to serve in your local church. Memorize Galatians 6:9. Of special note, this is my favorite verse. This verse reference is on the inside of my wedding ring and my wife's wedding ring.

WEEK 5

Isaiah 55:1–13
Focus: 55:8–9

Overview: Isaiah is encouraging the people of Israel to be restored to God through His mercy, love, and forgiveness. Isaiah says that we need to seek Him with a spiritual thirst and turn to Him. His Word is one way to have Him work in our lives. Through us and without us, His Word will accomplish His purpose (verse 11).

Focus: Verses 8 and 9 state that His ways and His thoughts are higher than our ways and our thoughts. His way is through Jesus Christ, who can forgive us and be the leader of our lives. His perspective is bigger than ours, and we need to try not to limit what He can do through us.

How to Apply: We will not always understand how He works, so we must allow our faith in Him to sustain us. Sometimes we need to let Him work. We can then join Him where He is working and not try our own ways. His Word can guide us, and we can pray beyond our plans and daily circumstances. A few good verses are Psalm 119:37, 105, and 133. Pray through these verses and Isaiah 55:8–9. Find a quiet place to pray and spend time in meditation—without asking Him for anything for yourself.

WEEK

6

Matthew 22:34–40
Focus: Matthew 22:37
Deuteronomy 6:1–9

Overview: Jesus responds to the question of the greatest commandment by stating that we are to love God first and then love our neighbors. In Deuteronomy, Moses receives the same answer for the people of Israel prior to their entrance into the promised land. The Old and New Testaments use terms like *mercy, forgiveness, salvation, guide, refuge, power, prayer, peace, faithfulness,* and *eternal life.*

Focus: But above all of these, as important as they are, God wants us to love Him first and put our relationship with Him first. In Matthew 22:37, He wants us to love Him with all of our hearts, souls, and minds. We have so many distractions throughout our days as we try to focus on loving Him first.

How to Apply: First John 5:21 states that we must keep ourselves from idols. With our relationship with Him first in our lives, we must remove any idol that gets in the way of knowing Him better. Pray through Matthew 22:37 and First John 5:21 and see what needs to be removed from your life because it is getting in the way of knowing God better.

WEEK

7

2 Chronicles 7:11–22
Focus: 7:14

Overview: Solomon finishes the temple and challenges Israel to turn from their wicked ways and return to God. Through their obedience to God, He will consecrate the temple and listen to their prayers. If they seek their own ways and other gods, He will uproot Israel from their land that He had given them. He will reject the temple and bring disaster on them.

Focus: Verse 14 tells us to "turn" toward Him through humility, prayer, and seeking Him. Humility is admitting He is sovereign, and it means being selfless in our lives. Prayer is talking to God on a regular basis to help us with our turning. Seeking Him is making a defined return to Him and shows that we are willing to remain obedient to Him.

How to Apply: Seeking Him is spending time in His Word to better know Him. Have a time of reflection this week to help your mind slow down from the daily grind, rut, routine, and rat race—and begin to turn. See Psalm 46:10. Spend time listening and in silence instead of just going on with your prayer requests.

WEEK
8

2 Chronicles 7:11–22
Focus: 7:14

Overview: This week, we will continue in verses 11-22. The challenge is to ensure our direction is from God. Reread verses 11-22.

Focus: God will forgive us and heal our relationship with Him, if we follow His instructions. For God's instructions, we will look at verse 14.

How to Apply: Humility is acknowledging His control in our lives and seeking His forgiveness and direction.

Prayer is talking to Him at a scheduled time and throughout the day. If your time is limited, start with at least five minutes per day. Include a written prayer list with specific requests.

Seeking means developing a thirst for Him to deepen your relationship with Him. Intentionally develop a daily reading plan in His Word. See 2 Timothy 3:16–17.

To turn is to make a decisive turn or change in our lives. Areas to change may include our attitudes, habits, thoughts, words, church attendance, Bible study, and relationships. Some may be gradual, and some may demand a turn today.

During this week, pray and ask God what area or two you need to work on this week.

WEEK
9

2 Timothy 4:1–22
Focus: 4:7

Overview: Paul challenges Timothy to continue to preach God's Word—to instruct, encourage, and rebuke those whom he is teaching. This is a follow-up to his prior verses in 3:16–17. Through His Word, we are "thoroughly equipped" and focused on His truth. Paul warns Timothy of people turning from the truth, seeking their own desires, and listening to teachers who tell them what they want to hear. Paul encourages Timothy to endure through the Lord's crown of righteousness in verse 8.

Focus: Our focus will be to fight, finish, and keep the faith with Paul as our example. Our reward is the crown of righteousness, which the Lord will award us the day we enter into eternal life with Him. Reading His Word keeps us focused on His sound doctrine. We need to read and apply His Word in our lives.

How to Apply: His Word will support us (Joshua 1:8), encourage us (Philippians 3:12–14), and guide us (Proverbs 3:5–6). One key is moving ahead in His strength (Isaiah 40:30–31). Review these verses and pick one to memorize this week. This will ensure that we are spending daily time in His Word and growing stronger in Him.

WEEK
10

2 Timothy 4:1–22
Focus: 4:7

Overview: For this week, we will continue in verses 1-22. Paul stresses that we need to be grounded in God's Word. This will keep us grounded in sound doctrine.

Focus: In verse 4:7, Paul tells us what his life has been focused on in order to obtain eternal life.

How to Apply: Paul focused on seeking God's perspective as we seek eternal life through Him. This can be easily missed when we get caught up in the daily issues and routine. Toward His crown of righteousness, Paul challenges us in verse 4:7:

- Fought: He has struggled and overcome through many joys and trials. In verse 4:17, Paul states God was always by His side.
- Finish: He has finished and completed God's purpose and plan for His life. Verse 4:17 states that the gospel was presented through Paul.
- Faith: Paul kept the faith even when he did not always understand or see God's big picture.

In our lives, we may not always understand or see His big plan or purpose. We can get lost in the craziness of our daily living. Spend some time in prayer this week. Pray about some current trial you are in and consider God using you in the future as part of a bigger perspective. Reread verses 4:7 and 4:17.

WEEK 11

Titus 2:1–15
Focus: 2:12

Overview: Paul encourages Titus to teach sound doctrine through the Word of God. He mentions self-control in verses 2, 5, 6 and 12. This is for all ages to be self-controlled, in order for us to remain focused and steadfast in following God. Titus was an example to others through his teaching, as God brought grace, forgiveness, and salvation for all men (verse 2:11).

Focus: In verse 12, Paul emphasizes saying *no* to ungodliness and worldly passions. We are to live self-controlled lives through time in His Word. Being grounded in His Word keeps us on track in following Him. Paul continues in verse 13, with looking ahead to our hope in the coming of Christ. Paul refers to this often to help us keep our perspective.

How to Apply: Consider an area of your life where God is telling you *no* and pray about it this coming week. Examples may include our thought life, our words, anger, envy of others, too much TV, not enough time in His Word and our attitudes. Pray through verses 2:12–14.

WEEK
12

Joshua 1:1–18
Focus: 1:8

Overview: Moses has passed on, and Joshua is working with God to lead Israel into the promised land. God's instructions include that God will not leave them. They must obey His Word and be "strong and courageous" (verses 6, 9 and 18). Israel has been wandering in the desert and will need to refocus and be strong as they move forward.

Focus: His challenge in verse 8 is that we must read His Word, meditate on it, and be obedient. This will bring us prosperity and success. His Word will continue to change our hearts to be more like Him. As we become more like Him and know Him better, our definitions of prosperity and success will match God's definitions.

How to Apply: Spend time in His Word this week. Start a daily reading program of ten minutes per day. Take verse 8 and pray through it to focus on His commands—strong, courageous, and obedient—and His promises to be with us in prosperity and success. Joshua 1:8 would also be a good memory verse.

WEEK 13

Psalm 1
Focus: 1:2

Overview: This psalm shows a contrast between the way of the righteous and the way of the wicked. The wicked will perish with God's wrath when they are judged. The blessed will delight in His Word. Through His Word, we are planted like a tree that prospers near water and does not wither. Again, as seen last week in Joshua, His Word will help us focus and prosper.

Focus: Verse 2 challenges us to meditate on His Word, think about it, love it, obey it, and use it in our prayers. Our foundation for wisdom, discernment, daily living, direction, and prosperity is built by reading His Word. Our goal is to spend daily time in His Word. Our delight should be in His Word.

How to Apply: This is a stretch week with a challenge to try to be more consistent in His Word. Read and meditate on a psalm per day, starting with Psalm 1 tomorrow. Follow up in the next five days with Psalms 3, 19, 34, 111, and 139. Write a key verse that jumps out to you from each psalm.

WEEK
14

1 John 2:1–17
Focus: 2:16

Overview: This is an encouragement from John to be obedient to our Father and to not live in sin but as someone who has the truth in Him. Our actions toward others should reflect Him living in us and show that we have come to know Him. By obeying His Word, God's love is made complete in us (verses 2:5–6).

Focus: Our love for Him and His love in us should keep our focus away from loving this world. We are in the world, but we need not be drawn into it and be controlled by worldly influences. Our caution in verse 16 is to keep away from our desires, sinful lusts, and pride in ourselves.

How to Apply: His Word will help us focus on His will and find peace and contentment in Him. During this week, review an area of your life that may be keeping you too close to the world. Work on a major change in areas including TV, time usage, thoughts, words, relationships, books, and movies. This may include increasing your daily prayer time and your Bible reading time, along with more consistent church attendance.

WEEK
15

1 John 3:11–4:6
Focus: 4:4

Overview: Continuing in 1 John, John encourages us to love one another, as God loves us. Our love should not just be with words or tongue, but supported with actions and in truth (verse 3:18). He repeats His challenge for us to be obedient to Christ and do what pleases Him. Through Him living in us, we will recognize false spirits, false teachers, and false prophets of this world. They are not of God; they are part of worldly desires, lusts, and pride from last week.

Focus: We can recognize worldly beliefs and seek His way because He has overcome the world. Verse 4:4 says it directly: "The one who is in you is greater than the one that is in the world." God has overcome the world.

How to Apply: Continue in the area of your life that you began to work on changing last week. Use verse 4:4 as a promise that God will help you conquer this area, so it will no longer control your life. Place this area to change on your prayer list. Verse 4:4 is a good verse to memorize.

WEEK
16

Proverbs 3:1–12
Focus: 3:5–6

Overview: The challenge from Proverbs 3 is to remember His teachings and obey them. Our priority is putting Christ first in all areas of our lives—not just at the top of your priority list but more like a wheel with spokes going out from the center for all areas of your life. Christ should be at the center of the wheel, touching all areas. Our focus over the past fifteen weeks includes His perspective, reading His Word, daily prayer time, and making changes (turns) in our lives.

Focus: The continued direction is to have complete trust in Him—even when we do not understand. We must acknowledge Him in all we do and continue to strive for His purpose for our lives to match His direction for our lives. Verses 3:1, 3 also stress the importance of memorizing His Word. Start with verses 5 and 6.

How to Apply: During this week, read, memorize, and pray through verses 5 and 6 every day:

- complete trust (verse 5a)
- not my way (verse 5b)
- His way (verse 6a)
- stay straight (verse 6b)

WEEK

17

Romans 12:1–21
Focus: 12:2

Overview: This chapter in Romans is about change. The word *transformed* is used in verse 12:2. Throughout this chapter, there are references to using our specific gifts for God, realizing we are each an important part of His church and ensuring that we do not think too highly of ourselves. Verses 9–12 include *moving forward, to serve Him,* and *to be faithful in prayer.* This chapter covers a list of multiple instructions to transform our lives.

Focus: These changes may have us trying to break some habits or patterns in our daily lives. Change is a process, and it starts through prayer by identifying areas in our lives that we need to turn. We can list all these instructions and work on them one at a time. Verse 12:2 tells us not to be conformed to the patterns of this world and to be transformed through the renewing of our minds (Colossians 3:2).

How to Apply: This coming week, allow God to transform you. Spend some time in prayer, review some of Paul's instructions, and identify patterns you need to change. Commit to praying ten minutes each day to start, using verse 12:2 as your prayer and as a great memory verse.

WEEK
18

Nehemiah 1:1–11
Focus: 2:4

Overview: In chapter 1 of Nehemiah, he was praying to gain an audience with the king to seek permission to return to Jerusalem and rebuild the walls. His brief prayer in verse 2:4b shows evidence of an ongoing prayer life. Reading the book of Nehemiah, we see him as a leader, organizer, communicator, encourager, intentional, planner, and man of prayer. His prayers in verses 5–11 give us a great format for our prayers, using ACTS:

Focus:

- Adoration (verses 5–6): Take time to first praise Him as an awesome God.
- Confession (verses 6–7): Cleanse our hearts through confession to God.
- Thanksgiving (verses 8–10): Thank Him for His promises, what He has given us, and salvation.
- Supplication (verse 11): Bring our specific requests before Him.

How to Apply: Pray this week using this format—along with a list of Bible verses to pray and a list of specific prayer requests.

WEEK 19

Philippians 4:1–23
Focus: 4:6, 7

Overview: In the first five verses, Paul encourages us to stand firm, rejoice in the Lord, and help our fellow believers. He continues through this chapter to tell us not to be anxious (6), recognize His peace (7), what to think on (8), learn to be content (12), and know our strengths (13) and needs (19) are through Him alone.

Focus: He can move us through all circumstances. Verses 4:6–7 talk of not being anxious as we come before Him in prayer. We are very selfish and usually want things in our timing and our way. Daily prayer can help us seek His way and help us wait for His timing. We will then know the peace that is beyond our understanding and which only He can give us.

How to Apply: This chapter has many good verses we can use to pray through: 4:6, 7, 8, 12, 13, and 19. During this week, pray through these verses and pick one to memorize. Add a request to your prayer list based on your review of these verses.

WEEK
20

Psalm 34
Focus: 34:13–14

Overview: This Psalm starts with praise to Him in verses 1–12. These verses work well as a prayer. He blesses those who take refuge in Him, He delivers those who fear Him (awe and reverence), and He takes care of those who seek Him. Verses 13–14 transition the psalm. Verses 15–27 explain that He is being attentive to and taking care of the righteous. He is against those who do evil and condemns the wicked.

Focus: Verses 13–14 contain active verbs that call us to action:

- *keep*—control our tongues (Ephesians 4:29)
- *turn*—decisive move away from evil actions
- *seek*—pursue peace

How to Apply: A challenge is to check how we use our words this week with others. We can intentionally use words to support and encourage instead of evil words, sarcasm, criticism, gossip, and insults. Use Psalm 19:14 to pray through and memorize.

WEEK 21

Hebrews 4:1–16
Focus: 4:12

Overview: God's Word can guide us to obedience and challenges us to examine our own lives to keep us on track in our walk with Him (Psalm 139:23-24). Hebrews 4:12 states His Word is sharp, penetrates our lives, judges our thoughts and attitudes, and uncovers all our disobedience and our weaknesses.

Focus: Christ is our source, and He understands us in our areas of temptation. He was subject to temptation while being a man, yet He did not sin. He can help us when we are tempted to disobey (Hebrews 2:18). Therefore, we can approach Him with confidence to His throne of grace and remain firm in our faith that we profess.

How to Apply: Verse 16 tells us that our confidence in Him and His Word will allow us to receive grace and mercy in our time of need. We can read His Word to expose our weaknesses. This will require a daily self-evaluation of where we are in our walk with Christ (Lamentations 3:40). Pray through and memorize Hebrews 4:16 this week.

1 Samuel 16:1–23
Focus: 16:7

Overview: God moves Samuel to anoint one of Jesse's sons to be king over Israel. Samuel passes over the first seven sons, and they wait for the youngest to come in from the field. The Lord chose David, a shepherd who was the youngest and smallest son. Samuel first saw the seven sons and thought one of them would be picked.

Focus: Verse 16:7 tells us that God does not consider physical appearance. Instead, He looks at the heart. He looks at our inner strength. He considers our character, attitude, willingness to serve, and commitment to Him. Man looks outwardly and comments or judges with no reference to his attitudes or thoughts.

How to Apply: As we continue to seek Him to build our relationship with Him, we must start with our hearts. Our hearts are what God sees. He is the one who searches our hearts. Reread verse 16:7. For this week, read, pray through, and memorize Psalm 139:23–24. Start with an evaluation of each of your days during this week.

WEEK
23

1 Samuel 17:1–54
Focus: 16:37, 45, and 47

Overview: Goliath of the Philistines frightened The Israelites. This is the story most of us know. David is just a boy and a shepherd. He comes in the name of the Lord and uses one stone and a slingshot to defeat Goliath. David knows his victory was through the Lord. Verse 17:47 explains that the battle belongs to the Lord. David trusted Him in the small things (if killing a bear and lion is small compared to a giant) and was used in a powerful way in killing Goliath.

Focus: God has not changed. He is the same God today who loves us, watches over us, guides us, and gives us victory. As He works through us, what are your expectations? Do we limit God with our prayers and actions? Our prayers must move us beyond our abilities and skills. We can do all things through Him (Philippians 4:13) and can do nothing without Him (John 15:5).

How to Apply: During this week, spend some time praying through 17:37, 45, and 47, Philippians 4:13, and Psalm 46:10. Where is God using you that you feel limited? Do you need to raise your expectations for what He can accomplish through you?

WEEK

24

Proverbs 4:1–5:2
Focus: 4:23

Overview: These verses remind us to seek wisdom and discernment in the paths we walk. We must spend time in His Word. We must read, meditate on, and obey His Word (4:20–21). We must be careful with our words, our heart, our steps, and our paths. All these are action verbs and tell us to continue to move forward and avoid the wicked.

Focus: His Word needs to be in our hearts as God examines our hearts and all our paths (Proverbs 5:21). Our paths include our words, thoughts, relationships, responsibilities, and avoidance or non-avoidance of the wicked. The way of the wicked will result in darkness. He pushes His point in verses 4:1, 20 and 5:1 ("pay attention").

How to Apply: Ask God to check and correct any areas of your path that may need help in turning back to Him. Pick a verse or two to pray through and memorize. Suggestions are Proverbs 4:20, 21, 23, 5:1 and 16:23.

WEEK
25

Psalm 139:1–24
Focus: 139:23, 24

Overview: David talks of God knowing the details of our lives. He knows our thoughts, our plans, and what we will say next. There is nowhere we can go to flee from His presence. No matter where we go, His hand is there to guide us and hold us fast.

Focus: Looking at verses 23 and 24, He knows and searches our hearts and anxious thoughts. As we evaluate ourselves, He can let us know if anything gets in our way of knowing Him better. Sometimes it is daily evaluation with confession and purifying of our hearts (1 John 1:9). Other times it is evaluating major issues in our lives to check for positive or negative influences or impact. Some of our idols (1 John 5:21) may include hobbies, friends, relationships, career, Facebook, or iPad time.

How to Apply: For this week, spend time to pray through verses 23 and 24 with the following:

- *know*—God knows us in detail
- *evaluate*—check for any offensive ways
- *remove*—any idol in our way of knowing God
- *lead*—follow in God's way

WEEK 26

Hosea 6:1–7:1
Focus: 6:3

Overview: Hosea talks of Israel's unfaithfulness and sinfulness. Verses 1–2 tell of returning to the Lord so He will heal and restore them. God has forgiven them, but they continue to disobey. Verses 6:4–7:1 tell of the wickedness and unfaithfulness of Israel. Verse 6 actually gives us a preview of Christ's death bringing in the new covenant from the Old Testament time of sacrifice and offerings to the New Testament of mercy and a relationship with God (Mark 12:33).

Focus: We, like Israel, sometimes are in the same pattern of returning to the Lord, forgetting about Him, disobeying again, and seeking restoration. Verse 3 tells us to press on to acknowledge and know Him. Key action words would be to "press on." He will respond and come as sure as the sun rises and the spring rains come.

How to Apply: We can seek daily forgiveness and restoration (1 John 1:9). Use 6:3 as a memory verse for this week. How can you press on to know Him better: daily prayer, consistent Bible reading, relationships for support, serving Him, or consistent church attendance?

WEEK
27

Psalm 42:1–11
Focus: 42:1, 2

Overview: This is a Psalm for a downcast soul. Sometimes we feel disturbed, depressed, weary in faith, or abandoned by God. This writer sees all this and feels that his life is absent from God's presence. How does he deal with his situation? He is honest with God about how he feels with his life. He remembers to continue to put his hope in Him and praise and worship Him (verses 5 and 11).

Focus: In the middle of his struggles, the writer prays that God will fill him with relief. Do not give up on God. As in verses 1–2, continue to long for God and thirst for God. These verses give a great picture of a deer panting and thirsting for water. We should work on seeking the living God.

How to Apply: When we seek and pursue God, His Word has many promises that we will find Him. Pray through these verses this week:

- our thirst for Him (Psalm 42:1, 2)
- our hope in Him (Psalm 42:5, 11)
- He will respond to us (Hosea 6:3)
- hope (Romans 15:13)

WEEK
28

1 Chronicles 16:11; Isaiah 55:6;
Matthew 26:41; Romans 12:12;
Colossians 4:2; and 1 Thessalonians 5:17

Overview: To continue from last week, we must thirst for Him, keep our hopes in Him, and grow our relationships with Him. When we work on human relationships, we spend time talking to that person. The same is with God—to spend time talking to Him through daily prayer. Our prayer time can take the form of praise and worship, praying through Bible verses, and prayer with specific requests.

Focus: These six verses encourage us to pray, to seek Him, and to be alert to pray throughout our days. Use these verses to begin to make prayer a priority in your life. God must be at the center of our lives and influencing every part and season of our lives. Prayer is an added part of our walk with God to influence our walk with Him and every part and season of our lives.

How to Apply: Meditate on these verses this week and start or continue your prayer request list. Include the date of the requests and the dates when they are answered. Start or continue to list Bible verses that you can use to pray through. Use one of these verses to be part of your Bible verse list.

WEEK
29

Matthew 6:1–18
Focus: 6:9–13

Overview: This chapter in Matthew is part of Jesus's Sermon on the Mount. He begins by telling us to give and pray in private and not to do publicly and seek credit from men (Galatians 1:10). When done in secret, God will know and will reward us. We need to pray specifically and not go "babbling like pagans" (verse 6:7).

Focus: In verses, 9–13, Jesus teaches us how to pray:

- through praise (verse 9)
- seeking His will (verse 10)
- asking for daily support (verse 11)
- forgiveness (verse 12)
- deliverance from temptation (verse 13)

How to Apply: During this week, pray through verses 9–13. Consider finding a quiet place in your house to come on your knees to pray (Luke 22:41, Psalm 95:6). This may be a room, a closet, or next to a specific chair. Include yourself, your family, and your church family in your prayers.

WEEK 30

Matthew 6:19–34
Focus: 6:34

Overview: We continue in chapter 6 of Matthew. Jesus gives us multiple instructions, including our priorities and our worries. He particularly mentions for us not to worry through examples of how God takes care of the birds of the air and the lilies of the field. He tells us we are much more valuable than the birds and the lilies.

Focus: In verses 19–34, in some key verses, Matthew challenges us to:

- keep our treasures toward heaven, with our focus on serving Him;
- serve and be devoted to God and not other idols (money) in our lives;
- not worry in our circumstances (Psalm 94:19) and grow our faith; and
- seek His kingdom first and know He will take care of us.

How to Apply: Seek His consolation this week to free our lives of worry. Evaluate any worry of current situations that will distract us from growing our faith and relationship with God. Verse 6:34 would be a great memory verse and good to pray through each day. Write the verse on an index card and place it on your bathroom mirror or car visor.

WEEK
31

Nehemiah 9:5–37
Focus: 9:31

Overview: Nehemiah was gathering the people to publicly pray to God. The wall around Jerusalem had been restored and completed. Through prayer, Nehemiah wants to restore their relationship with God. He is a man of prayer and realizes how much God was part of the rebuilding project of the wall. Man plans his course, but the Lord determines his steps and the outcome (Proverbs 16:1).

Focus: Nehemiah starts with worshipping and praising Him for who He is. He continues with thanking God for all He has done for Israel. This includes a brief history of being rescued from Egypt, parting the Red Sea, helping them survive in the desert, and taking their land from neighboring kingdoms and nations. God has shown His faithfulness to Israel.

How to Apply: For this week, spend time reading Nehemiah's prayer (9:5–15) and use it for praising Him. Make a list of twenty times God has been faithful to you and provided blessings in your life.

WEEK
32

Nehemiah 9:5–37
Focus: 9:31

Overview: Last week, we spent time praising and thanking Him. We continue this week in Nehemiah, finding the people of Israel did at times become arrogant and did not obey God's commands (9:16, 26). They would rebel, get into trouble, and cry for help, and God would rescue and restore them. God would still show His mercy and forgiveness for their actions.

Focus: In His forgiveness, God showed He is gracious and compassionate. He is slow to anger and abounding in love (9:17b). In His great mercy, He did not destroy them or abandon them (9:31). He loves us the same today and shows mercy to us—despite our tendencies to fall away from Him. When our lives are going well, we tend to drift until we need His rescue and forgiveness again.

How to Apply: For this week, study who He is through these verses to remember how He has not abandoned us when we feel we have turned away and disobeyed Him. Make this a week to see how much we can be thankful for in our lives. List fifteen things you are thankful for.

WEEK

33

Nehemiah 10:1–39
Focus: 10:29

Overview: Nehemiah's prayer begins with praises, blessing reminders, and seeing He is a merciful and loving God. He did not abandon them. In chapter 10, he concludes with challenging the people to obey God's Law, be obedient, and obey the regulations and decrees of the Lord. These include being separate from other nations, honoring the Sabbath, giving of offerings and tithes, and not neglecting the house of God.

Focus: Today we are not under the Law and—through Christ—our salvation gives us relationships with God. Our relationships with Him must grow. Our obedience should support growing our relationships with Him and include the actions mentioned below.

How to Apply: Pick one of the below actions, to work on this week:

- spending daily time in His Word
- attending weekly church
- honoring the Sabbath
- praying daily
- tithing our money
- tithing our time
- tithing our talents to serve

WEEK
34

Psalm 119:1–16
Focus: 119:9–11

Overview: Psalm 119 talks a lot about His Word. His Word is to be fully obeyed as we seek Him, walk in His ways, and pray that our ways will be steadfast. The writer uses different words for God's Word: obeying His ways, statutes, precepts, commands, and decrees. Look up Webster's definition for each of these words for valuable insights.

Focus: Through Webster, His Word would also be rules, directions, demands, and requirements. Verses 9–16 tell us to walk according to His Word. We can avoid straying or sinning against the Lord by hiding His Word in our hearts (verses 10–11). Memorizing His Word allows us to call verses to mind when we need them to encourage ourselves or encourage others. We can also pray through them.

How to Apply: Use Psalm 119: 9–11 to meditate on this week. Pray that His Word will keep you focused on Him, staying on His path, and that you would catch the writers' enthusiasm for His Word. Refer to Psalm 119:105.

WEEK
35

Psalm 119:33–40
Focus: 119: 36, 37

Overview: Psalm 119 gives us many challenges to seek His Word, to pursue Him, to follow His decrees, and to obey His commands. Last week, we noted the different words for His instructions to us from His Word. This week, referencing verses 33–40, we look at the action words directed to asking for help with His instructions. These verses can be used as specific requests to pray as you talk to God.

Focus: These requests include:

- teaching
- giving
- directing
- fulfilling
- preserving
- turning

One of the key words is *turn*. Verse 36 instructs us to turn our hearts toward His Word. Verse 37 challenges us to turn our eyes from worthless things.

How to Apply: What are the worthless things in your life right now: wasting time, sinning, impure thoughts, worthless words, wrong relationships, or selfish focus (119:36)? A *turn* dictates an intentional direction change to move us closer to God. Spend this week using these words in your prayer time with God and choose a worthless thing or two to eliminate from your life.

WEEK
36

Romans 8:1–27
Focus: 8:15

Overview: In this chapter, Paul talks of the sinful nature versus living a Spirit-controlled life. We must set our minds on what the Spirit desires. A mind controlled by a sinful nature is death. A mind controlled by the Spirit is life and peace. When we are controlled by our sinful nature, we cannot follow His will or please Him. The Spirit will intercede in our weaknesses to help us pray and follow His will (verses 26–27).

Focus: Through our salvation, we did not receive a spirit but the Spirit of God. Through His Spirit, we are no longer slaves to fear (Galatians 4:6–7, Romans 8:15). Being controlled by His Spirit helps us to be dead to sin while being alive in Christ. Our old sinful nature has gone, and our new nature is part of our new creation in Christ (2 Corinthians 5:17).

How to Apply: Ask God to help you be controlled by His Spirit during your daily prayer time this week. His Spirit will help you with your desires. As your relationship grows in Christ, your desires for your life will continue to better match what He wants and desires for your life. Pray through and memorize 2 Corinthians 5:17.

WEEK
37

1 Corinthians 2:1–16
Focus: 2:4–5

Overview: Paul came to preach the gospel and tell us about salvation through Christ. When we ask Him to be our Savior, He sends the Holy Spirit to dwell and live in us (John 14:16–17). Without the Spirit, nonbelievers and ourselves will not understand God's wisdom. We will not understand God's Word, His desires, and His character. When Paul first came to proclaim his testimony about God, he came with no eloquence as a speaker. He came in weakness, fear, and much trembling (2:4a).

Focus: He preached not on men's wisdom but on God's wisdom and a demonstration of the Spirit's power. Our faith must rely on God's power (2:4b, 5). The Spirit's wisdom is from God and helpful with our thoughts, words, and understanding Him more. Our life in Christ must be an example to those around us of our reliance on Him through all situations.

How to Apply: Pray that we are Spirit-filled people controlled by the Spirit in all our everyday choices and decisions. A simple example is my wife and I always wait one night and pray when we need to make a big decision. We do this even when we are told the plane ticket price, car price, or job offer will not be there if we wait until tomorrow!

WEEK
38

Colossians 1:1–23
Focus: 1:9–12

Overview: Paul encourages the church at Colossae as the gospel continues to be heard and the church continues to bear fruit and grow. The truth of the gospel rescues us from the darkness and brings us into His kingdom through His grace, redemption, and the forgiveness of our sins. Paul is thankful for them and continues to pray for Colossae as their faith grows from their hope in eternal life (1:3–5).

Focus: "Because" of verses 1–8, as summarized above, verse 9 tells us he has not stopped praying for the church. Verses 9–12 are good Bible prayers for ourselves and for our churches. Some repeated key words are *prayer* and *thankful*. Pray through these verses while using the following requests:

How to Apply:

- Be filled with knowing God through His Spirit.
- Live a life worthy of Him.
- Please Him in every way.
- Bear fruit in every work.
- Grow in your knowledge of God.
- Be strengthened with His power.

WEEK
39

Psalm 33
Focus: 33:20–22

Overview: Psalm 33 praises God for His creation—from the heavens to the seas. In verses 4–5, He tells of His characteristics including:

- His Word is right and true;
- He is faithful;
- He loves righteousness and justice;
- His unfailing love; and
- Praising Him for these characteristics can build our foundation on the hope we have through Him.

Focus: Verse 18 shares that the eyes of our Lord watch over those who fear Him and place their hope in Him. Verses 20–22 focus on this hope as our help and shield, as we trust in Him, with His unfailing love resting upon us. The word *hope* is used three times in these verses. Hope will renew our strength (Isaiah 40:31).

How to Apply: Reread verses 20–22, pray through them, and ask God to build your hope in Him. Hope is expectation and anticipation for our daily lives of living for Him and for our eternal lives of living with Him. We need to keep in God's love as we wait for Christ to bring us to eternal life (Jude 21).

WEEK
40

Hebrews 13:1–25
Focus: 13:25

Overview: The book of Hebrews tells us of God's overall plan for us and explains that we are an important part of the plan. Hebrews 11 is often referred to as the hall of faithful servants who have gone before us. They are an example to motivate us in serving the Lord and growing in faith. The book is full of specific instructions, including Jesus helping us through temptation (2:18), the power of His Word (4:12), drawing close to Him for help (4:16), knowing He can save us (7:25), and His faithfulness (10:23).

Focus: The final chapter (13) concludes with His final instructions and challenges to ensure we follow Him in all areas of our lives. There are twelve specific instructions that we can pray through in addition to the five references in the above overview.

How to Apply: Spend time praying through the above five references and the first four instructions in chapter 13:

- Continue to love others including strangers (13:1).
- Pray for all marriages (13:4).
- Pray for contentment (13:5a).
- Acknowledge that He is always with you (13:5b).

WEEK

41

Hebrews 13:1–25
Focus: 13:25

Overview: We will continue looking at the final instructions in Hebrews 13. These instructions in this chapter, will help us learn more about of the life we have in Christ and our role in God's plan through our influencing others around us. We reviewed and prayed through some last week.

Focus: Our focus is to pray specifically through the final eight (listed below). As you pray though them, consider their influence on your relationship with God and your relationship with others.

How to Apply:

- The Lord will help us (13:6).
- Jesus does not change (13:8).
- Pray for focused faith (13:9).
- Our citizenship is in heaven (13:14).
- Pray for our leaders (13:17).
- Pray for others (13:18).
- Pray He will equip us and His work in us will be pleasing to Him (13:21).
- His grace is where our salvation, our forgiveness, our relationship with Him, and our serving begin (13:25).

See Ephesians 2:8–10.

WEEK
42

Micah 7:1–20
Focus: 7:7

Overview: Micah talks about Israel struggling to obey God and the evil that has swept their land. Men are all evil, the upright are gone, and evil men wait in ambush. No one can be trusted. Families are against family members and their neighbors. A man's enemies are the members of his household. In the New Testament, Jesus mentions that He did not come for peace but that believers and nonbelievers in the same household will bring families apart (Matthew 10:34–35).

Focus: Verse 7 begins with *but*, which transitions into the balance of this chapter. Micah says he will hope in the Lord and wait for Him—and God will hear him. He warns his enemies not to gloat because God will forgive Israel and restore it as a nation. Through all of this, God will help Israel become the nation and people He desires them to be. Verse 18 states that God pardons and will forgive us of our sins.

How to Apply: Review verses 18–19 and meditate on these attributes of God:

- merciful
- compassionate
- forgiver

God loves us so much that sent His Son to die for our sins (Ephesians 2:8–10).

Jude 1–25
Focus: 20–23

Overview: Jude shares three examples of where there was evil and God eventually destroyed them. The Lord destroyed the Egyptians chasing after the Israelites, He destroyed Sodom and Gomorrah, and angels who did not believe in Him. All suffered the punishment of eternal fire.

Focus: Evil exists today, and the world is turning away from God. People will no longer follow His Spirit, and they only follow their ungodly desires (verses 17–19). Jude does not just warn us. He calls us to persevere on earth while we wait for our eternal rewards (verse 21).

How to Apply: To help keep our eternal perspective, He shares the following five ways in verses 20–23:

- build our faith
- pray in the Spirit
- wait for Him
- be merciful to the unbelievers
- work to save them

Pray through these this week and work on saving them. Add some names of unbelievers to your prayer list.

WEEK

44

James 1:1–27
Focus: 1:23–24

Overview: James is a very practical book with some specific instructions to live our lives in and through Him. We will cover the second half of this chapter (beginning in verse 19). James challenges us to manage our anger and to be good listeners. We must listen more and speak less. We must also listen to His Word and respond by becoming doers of the Word (verse 22).

Focus: Verses 23–24 talk of a man looking at his face in a mirror and immediately forgetting what he looks like when he walks away. We must look and prayerfully evaluate our lives. God will reveal where we need to make changes. We must do what He says and be obedient to His Word. One of James's tougher instructions is learning to control our tongues (verse 26, Ephesians 4:29).

How to Apply: Here is list of issues we can evaluate in our lives for this week.

- controlling our anger (verse 19)
- being doers (verse 22)
- controlling our tongues (verse 26)
- looking after orphans and widows (verse 27)
- being controlled by God and not by the world (verse 27)

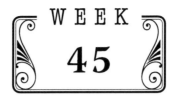

WEEK 45

Hebrews 10:1–18
Focus: 10:18

Overview: The first eighteen verses of Hebrews 10 review the covenant of the Old Testament. The people offered burnt offerings and sin offerings to the Lord for their sins and as a reminder of their sins. When Christ came into the world, He was the High Priest—and He died once for all. There are no longer any offerings needed or required for sin.

Focus: Jesus brought a new covenant to replace the old one. The new covenant brought forgiveness for our sins through His blood. God would grant complete forgiveness and would no longer remember our sins. We can grow our relationship with God and have our slates wiped clean of all our sins.

How to Apply: The new covenant is restated in the following verses. Read through these verses, particularly praying through Mark 12:32–33, to see how your love is complete with Him:

- 1 Samuel 15:22
- Hosea 6:6
- Hebrews 10:18
- Mark 12:32–33

WEEK

46

Hebrews 10:19–31
Focus: 10:24–25

Overview: From our review last week, Jesus opened a new and living way into a relationship with Him. We can be forgiven through His death. Forgiveness is granted when we commit and turn our lives completely to Him. Forgiveness is granted on a daily basis as we evaluate our lives each day and seek change.

Focus: Verses 22–25 talk of our relationship with God. They also mention our relationships with others. We can build our relationships with others through social times, Bible study groups, and regular church attendance. How do your commitments and schedules match against the above three areas? Is there a relationship in your life who you can encourage or who can encourage you?

How to Apply: Pray through the following verses to see where you may need to make adjustments in your walk with God:

- Draw near to God (verse 22)—relationship with God
- Hold to his hope (verse 23)—relationship with God
- Spur others on (verse 24)—relationship with others
- Encourage community (verse 25)—relationship with others

Proverbs 2:1–22
Focus: 2:10–11

Overview: These verses tell us of wisdom, which is one of the key topics in Proverbs. Verses 1–4 have *ifs* and challenge us to manage our lives as we seek Him and His Word. The more daily time we spend in His Word, the more we will know, understand, and obey in our walks with the Lord. Look at the word *turning* in verse 2 as we turn to hear His wisdom and make changes in our lives to seek His wisdom.

Focus: If we manage the ifs, His wisdom will help us deepen and grow our relationships with Him. He will guide us, guard us, and protect us like a shield. Look up the definition of wisdom. James 1:5 tells us to ask for wisdom—and He will generously give to us. This will happen with time in His Word.

How to Apply: Verses 10–11 summarize verses 1–9. Pray through these attributes of God and ask yourself how to develop a deeper hunger for His Word and relationship:

- wisdom
- knowledge
- discretion
- understanding

WEEK

48

Psalm 119
Focus: 119:166–176

Overview: Verses 166–176 are almost like a summary of Psalm 119. This is the longest psalm, and it challenges us to seek Him, delight in His Word, and know His Word. The writer challenges us to seek His wisdom and obey His commands and precepts. Also, this psalm will guide us, direct us, and show us how to follow His straight path (119:105).

Focus: This is a stretch week with a challenge to spend about fifteen minutes per day praying in His Word (using Psalm 119). Read some verses each day of the week as listed below and ask God to become more real in your life through His Word:

How to Apply:

    Day 1: verses 1–24
    Day 2: verses 25–48
    Day 3: verses 49–72
    Day 4: verses 73–96
    Day 5: verses 97–120
    Day 6: verses 121–144
    Day 7: verses 145–176

WEEK
49

Galatians 5:16–26
Focus: 5:25

Overview: Are we living by the Holy Spirit—or are we living and controlled by sinful nature? When Jesus rose to heaven, He left the Spirit with us as our Counselor and Helper. He will help us learn and remember what we have learned. God guided His people through the Old Testament with the law. Jesus taught through the New Testament that His death brings us salvation. He left the Holy Spirit for us today until His coming.

Focus: Paul knew the Holy Spirit was important since He discusses the contrast of the Spirit and people's sinful nature in a number of His books. Jesus knew the Holy Spirit was an equal part of the Trinity: Father, Son, and Holy Spirit. Paul gives us two contrasting lists to review in Galatians 5.

How to Apply: Pray through the two lists below and check off one from each list to work on changing the impact in your life:

- sinful nature (verses 19–21)
- fruit of the Spirit (verses 22–23)

WEEK
50

1 Peter 1:1–25
Focus: 1:13–15

Overview: Peter talks of us living here in our world in verses 1–12. We have a new birth and a living hope in our salvation through His death and resurrection. We may suffer some trials at times, but this helps our faith grow and become stronger and more genuine. A genuine faith will result in praise and worship of Christ and giving Him the glory. Our joy for Him works through faith, and our true goal is our salvation.

Focus: *Therefore*, beginning in verse 13, we must continue to see the big picture of looking to eternal life with Him. This *therefore* transitions us from knowledge to action. Our lives must be directed by our hopes that are set on Him. Our hope is through His Word, which will stand forever (1:24–25).

How to Apply: Peter leaves us with the following instructions in verses 13–15. Review this week and prepare your minds for action (Philippians 4:8):

- Prepare your minds.
- Be self-controlled.
- Set your hope on Him.
- Do not conform to this world.
- Be holy.

WEEK
51

2 Peter 1:1–21
Focus: 1:4

Overview: Peter's introduction advises us not to limit God. Through our knowledge of God, He wishes us grace and peace in abundance. Peter continues to talk of His divine power, which provides everything we need to live for life and godliness. This is through our knowledge of Him and knowing Him (verse 3). We can participate in His divine power and escape the corruption and evil desires of this world (verse 4).

Focus: In verse 5, Peter transitions us into a list of qualities that are not part of a new message. We have seen these before, but they are important. We must live these qualities in a growing measure so we will be effective and productive as we live to know God more each day. A *therefore* in verse 10 tells us to be sure of our calling and know His purpose for our lives.

How to Apply: These qualities will help us receive a rich welcome into His eternal kingdom. Be intentional to ensure that these following qualities are being lived and grown in your life:

- faith
- goodness
- knowledge
- self-control
- perseverance
- godliness
- brotherly kindness
- love

Pray through all of them and record two specific qualities to adjust or strengthen in your walk with God.

WEEK 52

Exodus 5:1–22
Focus: See below

Overview: Exodus 3 tells of Moses receiving His calling from God through a burning bush. God has heard the cries from the people of Israel being oppressed in Egypt. He will come down to rescue them out of the land of Egypt and bring them to the promised land, which is flowing with milk and honey (3:7–8). God tells Moses He is sending him to bring His people out of Egypt. Have you ever been hesitant to obey God? Does the task or job seem too big and beyond your abilities?

Focus: Moses's first response was to ask, "Who am I to be able to accomplish this assignment?" Moses questioned God seven times that he could not do this, but God still used Moses in a powerful way to start and finish his assignment.

How to Apply: This is a stretch week with multiple verses to look up. Pray through these verses for obedience to God through His strength and wisdom:

- Exodus 3:11, 13; 4:1, 10, 13; 5:22–23; and 6:12

Pray through these verses for encouragement through Him:

- Ephesians 3:20; Proverbs 16:9, 19:21; Philippians 4:13; and 1 Corinthians 2:2–5

Biblical References

Week 1: 2 Timothy 1:1–18

Week 2: Ephesians 3:1–21

Week 3: Jeremiah 29:1–23

Week 4: Galatians 6:1–18

Week 5: Isaiah 55:1–13

Week 6: Matthew 22:34–40

Week 6: Deuteronomy 6:1–9

Weeks 7 and 8: 2 Chronicles 7:11–22

Weeks 9 and 10: 2 Timothy 4:1–22

Week 11: Titus 2:1–15

Week 12: Joshua 1:1–18

Week 13: Psalm 1

Week 14: 1 John 2:1–17

Week 15: 1 John 3:11–4:6

Week 16: Proverbs 3:1–12

Week 17: Romans 12:1–21

Week 18: Nehemiah 1:1–11

Week 19: Philippians 4:1–23

Week 20: Psalm 34

Week 21: Hebrews 4:1–16

Week 22: 1 Samuel 16:1–23

Week 23: 1 Samuel 17:1–54

Week 24: Proverbs 4:1–5:2

Week 25: Psalm 139:23, 24

Week 26: Hosea 6:1–7:1

Week 27: Psalm 42:1–11

Week 28: 1 Chronicles 16:11, Isaiah 55:6, Matthew 26:41, Romans 12:12, Colossians 4:2, 1 Thessalonians 5:17

Week 29: Matthew 6:1–18

Week 30: Matthew 6:19–34

Weeks 31 and 32: Nehemiah 9:5–37

Week 33: Nehemiah 10:1–39

Week 34: Psalm 119:1–16

Week 35: Psalm 119:33–40

Week 36: Romans 8:1–27

Week 37: 1 Corinthians 2:1–16

Week 38: Colossians 1:1–23

Week 39: Psalm 33

Weeks 40 and 41: Hebrews 13:1–25

Week 42: Micah 7:1–20

Week 43: Jude 1–25

Week 44: James 1:1–27

Week 45: Hebrews 10:1–18

Week 46: Hebrews 10:19–31

Week 47: Proverbs 2:1–22

Week 48: Psalm 119

Week 49: Galatians 5:16–26

Week 50: 1 Peter 1:1–25

Week 51: 2 Peter 1:1–21

Week 52: Exodus 5:1–22

Printed in the United States
By Bookmasters